THE
Rebirth
OF ME:
MY JOURNEY, BREAKTHROUGH
& TRIUMPH

A Hands-On Guide to Rebirth and a New Life

EBONY J. POTTS

Book Cover Design: Prize Publishing House

Printed by: Prize Publishing House, LLC in the United States of America.

First printing edition 2022.

Prize Publishing House
P.O. Box 9856, Chesapeake, VA 23321
www.PrizePublishingHouse.com

ISBN (Paperback): 979-8-9858926-1-1
ISBN (E-Book): 979-8-9858926-2-8

Contents

Dedication

This book is dedicated to that little girl from an urban area who had so many odds stacked against her. It's for the girl who one day decided that she was not going to be a statistic and wanted more out of life, so she believed that God could do it for her. This is for you, little Ebony.

Preface

I never imagined I would be here at this very moment writing, trusting God, and sharing my story, one that haunted me and made me feel too ashamed and afraid to share. Even at this moment, I am unsure what the future holds and what will come out of this moment in time, this leap of faith. But I do know one thing for certain: God assured me He will see me through this to the end and that my story will save someone's life. It may very well be you, the one touching the page. I appreciate you taking this leap of faith with me.

I want to also dedicate this book to you and every person who finds themselves in a season of searching. Perhaps you are searching for the right answers, searching for a sign, or even searching for something to stop you from jumping off the edge. Pretty please, don't give up yet. Take this journey with me through these pages and let God do the rest. There is purpose in your pain. Let me share with you my journey, breakthrough, and triumph and you will see just how similar our stories are. If God can do it for me, I pinky promise that He can do the same for you. You are closer than you think. I promise to be transparent, vulnerable, honest, and real. The purpose of this book is solely to share my story with the faith that it can save a life and bring God glory. This one's for you. Breathe in faith. Exhale fear. Let's do this!

Beauty from Ashes

"Before I formed you in the womb I knew
you, before you were born I set you apart; I
appointed you as a prophet to the nations."

JEREMIAH 1:5 (NIV)

Who am I? I don't blame you for wondering. I am going to let the pages answer that question, but I would like to start by explaining who I lived life *thinking* I was. I thought I was a nobody. I thought I was just a girl taking up space whom no one truly loved or wanted. I thought because my mom and dad chose drugs and that lifestyle over being a parent that there must have been something wrong with me. I wanted to be the fix that they so desperately craved. I yearned to be the itch they had when their subconscious told them to get another taste. I wanted so badly to be their only addiction, but I could never deliver that to them, so I lived life at an early age feeling like a failure. I never really understood what to do to get them, then eventually friends and men, to love me. I always thought that if I did one more thing, whether it be getting straight As, cooking a meal, or giving anything and everything away (my body, my dreams, my imagination, my hopes) to someone, then eventually they would love me. I thought I was damaged goods. I thought that being raped and molested at the age of five meant I must grow up. I thought I was stupid to believe in anything other than the reality that constantly slapped me in the face regularly: the reality of poverty, hunger, abandonment, etc. I had to learn how to get through each passing moment without a complaint, tear, or acknowledging any true pain I was feeling. I buried it deep down so well that I perfected a smile. I perfected maturity. I perfected being "wise beyond my years".

At the tender age of five, I lost so much. I played with the idea of just being a child like my peers when in reality I studied the adults around me and fell into a particular role. I began to think that I was never meant to be loved. I thought I was never allowed to be carefree. I thought adulthood had to begin at 5, especially since only adults have sex, right? So, I thought I must be one of those since I was already sexually active (not by choice). I thought this was just how it was and was going to be and that God Himself did not love me enough to help. I thought I'd figured something out. I realize now that I did figure out one thing and that was survival. I told myself: *"Smile just enough. Laugh just enough. Pretend you don't hear or understand the conversations around you. Be polite. Be smart. Work hard, but not at your dreams because you don't know what those are. You just know what others get excited about and what they love. So give them that at all costs."* I did not know the impact that this thinking would have on me later on in life and how it all came at a price. All of these thoughts and themes that I began to build brick by brick from adolescence to adulthood would eventually need to burn to the ground. What I can tell you now is that yes, it all came burning down, BUT God made beauty from those ashes and birthed something new. Well, not necessarily new; it was a REBIRTH.

Rebirth is defined by Webster's Dictionary as spiritual regeneration. God had a way of re-birthing me into who He originally created me to be: the Ebony before the molestation, before the rape, and before the abandonment of her parents. I returned to the Ebony before the mental and emotional abuse later endured in a marriage, and the Ebony before friends walked away and stones were thrown at her. He rebirthed that pure-hearted vessel, the Ebony who got buried deep down in a place so dark. The truest version of Ebony is what resurrected from those ashes. Let's talk about the journey back to that Ebony and all it required and entailed. It was not pretty, trust me. I realize it was never supposed to be.

There was purpose, favor, anointing attached to the pain of then, the pain of what came after, and the healing I am experiencing right now in this very moment as I write this. There is an indescribable joy I have because God has a way of working ALL THINGS out for our good. Want to hear how He did and is doing just that for me? Keep reading.

CHAPTER TAKEAWAYS

- As humans, we all may battle with becoming who the world desires us to be over who God created us to be.
- There is beauty in ashes. Even the ugliest moments in our lives can be instrumental in the process of becoming who we were created to be!
- Rebirth is defined as: "spiritual regeneration"

Processing Time: Use this page to journal
your thoughts, takeaways, etc.

_____

_____

_____

_____

_____

_____

_____

_____

_____

_____

_____

_____

_____

_____

_____

_____

_____

_____

_____

_____

_____

_____

_____

God's Will vs. My Will

*"'For I know the plans I have for you," declares
the LORD, "plans to prosper you and not to harm
you, plans to give you hope and a future.'"*

JEREMIAH 29:11 (NIV)

*H*is plans. Let's start there. God promises us that He already has plans for us and they are for good and not evil. He desires for us to have hope and a future. I grew up hearing and reciting this verse in church, but never truly believing the promise it entails. I functioned my entire life up until this very moment living out my plans. I subconsciously re-wrote that verse in my head and it sounded more like this: *"God, listen, here is what I am going to accomplish at this age. I am going to get married, I am going to buy a house, I am only going to take jobs giving me a certain amount of money, these are going to be my friends forever, I am going to have children by this age, and I just need you, God, to get on board, okay?"*

I planned my future out from start to finish, so much so that I remember even receiving a superlative award for being the "Fortune Teller" the summer of my sophomore year in college. I was always viewed as ambitious and goal-oriented by those I crossed paths with and I wore those titles like a badge of honor, not realizing the determinant in it spiritually. I pretty much played God and told Him, the creator of heaven and earth, what I was going to do and when I was going to do it; He just needed to join the party. I realize now that I never truly sought out His guidance, discernment, or direction, so although I did check off most of my boxes by obtaining the degrees, the money, the positions, the man, the friends, the house, and everything else, I was not fulfilled. I realize now that everything that I accomplished, every milestone met within my timeline hurt me in the end instead of fulfilling me because I did not involve Him in any of it. I would thank Him for the blessings but in reality, I was playing His role so much that it left me burnt out, stressed out, depressed, and subjected to a life where my spirit was breaking bit by bit. I was losing the Ebony He created in my mother's womb and masking it with accolades, degrees, and social media posts.

Eventually, all of which I planned according to the will of Ebony and not God's, He stripped away. The friends, the marriage, the house, the money, and the positions, were all gone. When this happened, I was sick. I had just separated from my husband. In the process of divorce proceedings along with court proceedings for a restraining order against him, friends whom I considered sisters turned away from me and many people judged me. I also had to sell my home, look for a new place to live, and make ends meet after accepting a new position with a 20k pay cut. The list goes on. I needed God more than ever before and He needed something from me too - my heart.

I came across a great site called FutureMe.org a few years ago. During this challenging moment in my life as God was preparing my rebirth, I received a letter from the past. I would like to share it with you and also encourage you to write letters to your future self as well because there's nothing God can't do.

*The following is an email from January 11, 2021,
delivered from the past by FutureMe.*

Dear FutureMe,

**While writing this you aren't feeling the best. You just tried to end it
all a week ago. You still haven't returned to work. Things seem dark.
I hope that the person reading this is in a happier place. If you are
I'm glad, Ebony. Remember all things are temporary. Please work
on you and try your hardest to push through this life. Whether it's a
new career or marriage. Work to find your happiness. I hope you're
doing better, future self because this dark place is nowhere to be.**

It was the immeasurable pain and hurt that I was experiencing as God
removed so much that brought me to my knees and I cried out this prayer:
"God, I am sorry for doing things my way. Obviously, my way was not it. I
give You full reign. You know far better than I do. I'm done being in control. Forgive me. Take the wheel. None of me and all of You. I don't know
what the future holds for me, but I know You promised that the plans You
have for me are not to harm me, but for me to prosper and to have hope
and a future. I need Your healing and Your way. I am ready!"

In that moment, God met me, and I want to share that even in your situation and your life journey there needs to come a point when you submit
to the will of God and give your life to Him. I am here to help you in any
way I can by giving you tips and strategies that worked for me along the
way. I call it my spiritual prescription. Just like any doctor whom you visit
when sick and prescribes you medication, I went to the Ultimate Physician.
He whipped out His pad and wrote me this prescription which has helped

medicate me and healed me from all hurt, pain, bitterness, and anger. I would love to share this with you and for you to pull from this; it'll help you through your rebirth.

Spiritual Prescription:

1. **Start the morning with God:** I woke up 30 minutes earlier each day. Before I did anything, I spent time meditating, praying, doing positive affirmations, and reading devotional plans. Here's what I used:
   - I started the morning with the Lord's Prayer (Matthew 6:9-13).
   - I used the Calm App (available for download on all devices) to help guide me in meditation.
   - I downloaded the YouVersion Bible App for Bible reading (available for download on all devices – it's a brown Bible icon).
   - I used the I Am App (available for download on all devices) to help guide me with daily affirmations.

2. **Listen to the Word of God:** Every morning after my 30 minutes of prayer and devotional time, I would listen to a sermon and have it playing while I showered and got ready for work. I typically listened to:
   - Pastors Sarah Jakes Roberts & Tourè Roberts of The Potter's House (available on YouTube).
   - Pastor Shavon Smith (Facebook & Spotify). I would tune in to her Cyber Church and podcasts regularly.
   - After a few days, I began to just ask God for a word, then opened YouTube and clicked on the first sermon that popped up. I always said, "Lord, please provide me with a word, one that You know I need to feed my spirit. Thank You in advance". I promise you, He ALWAYS delivered.

3. **Video Diaries:** Once every few days or weeks I would do a diary similar to writing in a journal, but instead I would prop my phone up and talk because it saved me time. I created a folder and saved them. I recorded on good and bad days. Writing in a journal works just fine. Either way, it is good to document your journey.

4. **Therapy:** I have an amazing therapist who also happens to be Christian, which matters to me. I am a huge advocate for therapy. It saves lives. You can't process things alone.

5. **Exercise:** I developed a gym routine. It does not have to be anything major, but endorphins are real!

6. **Eat Right:** I made sure to feed myself enough vegetables and protein and drink plenty of water. Your body needs nutrients and love.

7. **Sleep:** I got very serious about the amount of sleep I was getting at night. You can't be at your best when you are tired.

8. **Update Your Playlists:** I did my best at only listening to songs that made me feel good and fed my spirit. For me, gospel music does just that, but I also love some positive India Arie and Lauryn Hill. Be mindful of what you listen to because that feeds your spirit. The same goes for shows; I had to cut out shows that were toxic and made me feel anything less than good after viewing.

9. **Fasting:** I learned more about spiritual fasting. I participated in a few fasts, some that involved food restrictions and others where I gave up things I loved for some time, such as social media, drinking, and smoking marijuana. I wanted to approach my season of re-birth with a clear mind with very few distractions.

10. **Tithing:** I decided to give God what He asks in terms of my finances. I gave 10% of all earnings to Him by giving what I call seed offerings to ministries I felt were fruitful and helping my journey (i.e Shavon, SJR, and PT).

11. **Give Yourself Permission to Feel:** I did not fight my feelings or emotions. If I needed to cry, I cried. If I wanted to laugh, I did just

that. Allow yourself to be human and feel the emotions. Just don't stay with the negative, but always chase the light.

12. **Surround Yourself with Love:** I made an effort to only be around people who love me, whether it was family, trusted friends, kids I worked with, or animals. Where the love was, so was I. Protect your space.

CHAPTER TAKEAWAYS

- Submit to God. Give Him your heart. (If you never gave your life to Christ, you still can. I suggest praying this: *"Dear Jesus, I'm praying this prayer because I know that I have done wrong by living without You. I am sorry and I trust that You will forgive me. I accept Your love and grace for me and ask that You would be my Lord. Help me believe in You and love You every day and help me to show the world what You are like and how great Your love is. In Jesus' name, amen."* (https://hillsong.com/jesus/)

- God's plans are better than our own.

- Consider writing letters to your future self as this helps remind you of God's work. (FutureMe.org)

- A 'Spiritual Prescription' can help with your journey.

Processing Time: Use this page to journal your thoughts, takeaways, etc.

_____

_____

_____

_____

_____

_____

_____

_____

_____

_____

_____

_____

_____

_____

_____

_____

_____

_____

_____

_____

The Unwanted vs. The Wants

"Have I not commanded you? Be strong and courageous.
Do not be afraid; do not be discouraged, for the Lord
your God will be with you wherever you go."

JOSHUA 1:9

Let's keep journeying along together. While writing this God, has been revealing more and more of Himself and I believe in the power of His word. I hope you got a good laugh at how I pretty much was functioning all my life trying to be my own God. I shake my head at myself and laugh thinking, "Oh you thought you were doing something, huh?". I have been listening to and blessed by the ministry of Mrs. Sarah Jakes Roberts, or SJR for short (check her out - you will not regret it). I will periodically quote her, calling them SJR gems. God spoke through her to me and made me realize that I was so dead set focused on what I wanted out of life and all the plans I made that I refused to confront the unwanted.

Let's talk about the unwanted. I knew what I wanted out of life: the career, the degrees, the family, the husband, the money, and the community. But God pushed me to confront the very things that happened in my life that were unwanted and the things that I did not want to do. It is pushing through the unwanted that helps produce all that God wants for me, thus later giving me those wants. However, if we lock in solely on our wants and push away all the unpleasant unwanted things, moments, lessons, etc., we can never fully produce. In actuality, it is the unwanted stuff that requires just as much attention, blood, sweat, and tears that I was putting into achieving all the wants in my life/future. I hope this is not confusing you, but if it is, I promise it will make more sense if you keep rocking with me.

I sat with myself and made a list of all the unwanted things that have transpired thus far in my life. That became the list of *things I needed to confront*. Then, I made a list of all the things I did not want to do (the things that I honestly roll my eyes at and twist my face up about). That list is now what I would like to consider *my divine tasks to complete*. Let's walk this out together. Grab something to write with and a piece of paper. Divide that paper in half and title each side accordingly. I did promise you that I would keep it honest, real, and transparent earlier, right? So, here we go. Here's an example of my paper:

The things I did NOT want:	The things I do NOT want to do:
• Rape	• Forgive those who hurt me
• Molestation	• Have difficult conversations with certain family and friends
• Abandonment	
• Fear	• Go back to school
• Abuse	• Share my story/testimony
• Insecurity	• Face challenges/failures
• Divorce	• Help my family
• Infidelity	• Be patient
• Suicide attempts	• Relocate
• Hospitalizations	• Let go of certain habits
• Heartbreak	• Walk away from certain relationships
• Anxiety	
• Depression	• Be abstinent/celibate
• Betrayal	
• Judgment	
• Shame	
• Therapy	

The things I did NOT want:	The things I do NOT want to do:
• The decrease in salary & career change • Eating disorder • Addiction • Medications • A diagnosis	

Get your lists together. Take your time. You may even need to come back to add things and that is okay, too. Now, let's examine our lists. I don't know about you, but for me when creating my lists, I experienced two completely different sets of emotions. While writing on the left side I felt sadness, uneasiness, and a sense of "these things sucked". Memories attached to certain words even came flashing into my mind. As I began writing the right side of my list, I found myself having a little tantrum. I felt annoyed, angry, and wanted to scream "Lord I don't want to! Please don't make me" (add the eye rolls, sucking of the teeth and I even almost broke the tip of my pen). I had to wooosssaaahhh.

So, we have our list now. It was with these lists that I felt a breaking in my spirit. I felt God breaking off all of that from the right and giving me direction through the left side of my list along with a promise that He is going to be with me wherever I go, but that I must be strong and courageous. Do I still want certain things? Most definitely. I still want the home, husband, kids, career, etc. BUT what makes the Ebony from chapter two different from this Ebony is that I realize I cannot allow my wants to cause me to be blinded (thanks SJR). I must confront the unwanted things that have happened in my life and the things I don't even want to do because they are more important than all the things I want. All these unwanted pieces and wants must come into perfect harmony to birth something new, well actually to orchestrate my re-birth.

You are not alone in this process. God is right beside you and even when you don't feel Him, please know He is hovering; so be strong and courageous! I believe in us and I believe in the power of God. This re-birth does not feel good. I don't have children yet so I never experienced labor pains, but I do hear the stories and see the videos. It is not a pleasant sight and I'm sure every mom can attest to the pain, but in the same breath, they can attest to the joy that comes after the pain. Are you ready for your re-birth? Just breathe and let's keep journeying along. You got this and I am so proud of you already.

CHAPTER TAKEAWAYS

- The unwanted things of life and our wants have to come into harmony with one another.
- God can use all that we've been through and direct/guide us as we embark on doing what He requires.
- Be strong and courageous! God is here with you and will help you through this journey.

*Processing Time: Use this page to journal
your thoughts, takeaways, etc.*

4

Come out of Hiding

*"But he said to me, 'My grace is sufficient for you, for
my power is made perfect in weakness.' Therefore I
will boast all the more gladly about my weaknesses,
so that Christ's power may rest on me."*

2 CORINTHIANS 12:9 (NIV)

et's talk about weakness. Let me start by saying this: no one is perfect. I know we hear it all the time and even say it but for some reason, we still function as if this cliche is not true. Only Jesus himself was perfect so before we dive into this next chapter can we say this aloud together, I - AM- NOT- PERFECT!! I don't know about you, but that felt good and I felt something lift off of me. If you need to keep saying it out loud to yourself until you feel a shift and begin believing it, that's okay. I'll wait (I'm not going anywhere and this book isn't either; you bought it *wink*).

During this re-birth, I was made to see that I had been hiding. I even hid from myself so well that it took some time for me to even grasp this concept of hiding. I had to ask God, what do you mean I am hiding, I'm right here talking to you every day, so clue me in. What am I hiding? You know He answered, right? Not only did He answer, but He encouraged me to sit with Him and peek my little head out from my hiding place, and then my arm, a leg, and next thing you know I am fully exposed. Now, let me be honest with you, this did not feel good one bit, but He also reminded me that the very things aka insecurities and weaknesses I am hiding are the very things He wants to use.

Let's walk this out together. Go ahead and get your writing utensil and paper (I recommend getting a journal at some point to keep all your notes in one place). Ready? Okay, now together we are going to make another list, but this one is going to be a list of our insecurities/weaknesses (all that we hide). I wouldn't ask you to do anything I haven't already done, so here is my list for an example and guidance:

I am hiding …
• My past battles with depression, anxiety, and self-harm
• Past suicide attempts and hospitalizations
• My past with psychiatric medications
• My past battle with self-image, bulimia, and anorexia athletica
• That I was raped and molested on different occasions through adolescence and teenage years
• My learning challenges with processing information at times, spelling, and reading
• My testimony
• My shame of divorce and infidelity
• My experience with emotional and mental abuse from loved ones
• My healing
• My biggest dreams/goals
• My worth
• My voice

I realized that I thought I was just hiding these insecurities, shortcomings, and life events from the world (i.e family and friends), but I was also hiding them from God. I was going to God in prayer, but very surface level. Telling him just enough but not sharing the areas of my life I was not proud of. I was trying to keep God out of my business okay! But let me tell you this, God can't use what we refuse to uncover.

Once I began to come out of hiding I was finally able to go deeper in God and he pulled me to a whole new level. A level where I started to embrace the parts of me that didn't make me feel small (thanks SJR for another gem). I then got a new perspective of me, a new dimension of my re-birth. I began to change my frame of thinking and God began to heal the innermost parts of me which involved everything on that list and the ugly things that were attached to them such as fear, shame, doubt, low self-worth, etc. He worked with me on getting rid of that toxic habit I had of reminding myself of who I used to be or the things I endured. I had to stop because each time I was taking positive steps forward those negative reminders would pull me and hold me back from where I felt God wanted to take me. Yes, I've hurt people while I was hurting. Yes, I did not always make the right choices. Yes, I endured pain, heartache, and abuse, BUT you want to know what I did (I strongly encourage you to guess)? I began to hold those thoughts captive and spoke the word of God over them. I began to stop believing and trusting my thoughts and emotions and instead replaced them with what God said. God gave me a new list and this list is yours too!

God says:

- ❖ I am beautifully and wonderfully made. (Psalm 139:14)
- ❖ I am more than a conqueror. (Romans 8:37)
- ❖ I am a new creature in Christ. (2 Corinthians 5:17)
- ❖ I am not condemned by God. (Romans 8:1)
- ❖ I am strong and can do anything. (Philippians 4:13)
- ❖ I am free from the law of sin and death. (Romans 8:2)
- ❖ I am a fellow heir with Christ. (Romans 8:17)
- ❖ I am enough. (2 Corinthians 12:9)

It is hard to break old habits, especially the ones that aren't visible and live in our heads, but the same power that raised Jesus from the grave is the same power within you and me. I started speaking positively about myself over and over and over again until it became a new habit (studies show it takes 21 days for something to become a habit). Here is a challenge I want to give you that worked and continues to work for me. I want you to begin reciting who God says you are every day for the next 21 days. You can use the list above or even create your own. I used that list and then something I came across during my devotional plan that reads:

"I am beautiful, capable and worthy. I am made new in Christ. I was not given a spirit of fear, but of love, power, and a sound mind. I am more than a conqueror in Christ who gives me strength" (YouVersionBibleApp).

It is time for you to take on a new identity. Can I pray for you?

> *Dear Lord Jesus,*
>
> *You are an amazing Father. You see all things and know all things. You know all of our hiding places and still remain patient with us. Forgive us for pushing You aside and for never truly giving you all of us. I thank You for Your forgiveness, patience, love, grace, and mercy. I come to You interceding on behalf of this reader. Make Your presence known and help them to learn and embrace who You say they are. Help them to take on the identity You so carefully crafted. Help them along this journey and allow them to feel Your presence. Give them peace that transcends all understanding and help them to walk with their heads held high. Help them to know that others along with their circumstances do not define them, for You already told them through Your word who they are. Help them to dive deeper into You and protect them from the lies of the enemy. I thank You, Lord, for all that You have done, all that You are doing, and all that is to come.*
>
> *In Jesus' name,*
> *Amen.*

CHAPTER TAKEAWAYS

- Only Jesus is perfect and we are made perfect in him.
- God is waiting for us to come out of hiding and tell Him everything that haunts us.
- God sees us differently than the world may see us. Learn who God says you are and reject all other labels for they are lies.
- Take on a 21-day challenge getting rid of toxic habits and starting new ones.

Processing Time: Use this page to journal
your thoughts, takeaways, etc.

_____

_____

_____

_____

_____

_____

_____

_____

_____

_____

_____

_____

_____

_____

_____

_____

_____

_____

_____

_____

5

Time to Breakup

"Remember not the former things, nor consider the things of old. Behold, I am doing a new thing, now it springs forth, do you not perceive it?"

ISAIAH 43:18-19 (NIV)

The past is like that pesky little fly or mosquito at the cookout that just won't let you enjoy your mac and cheese. It keeps buzzing in your ear or biting at your flesh when all you want is some peace! The past and the pain attached to it can be very annoying, like those insects. But have you ever thought about how eventually you adapt and grow accustomed to the past and pain? You may even use the phrase "it is what it is". That phrase forces us to accept things for what they are and also accept that they will always be that way so eventually you give up trying to kill that fly or mosquito and learn to live with it. The flip side to that which I later realized is that subconsciously not only did I learn to live with the pain I even began to find comfort in it. Am I the only one? It's like we can grow used to the pain and grow in relationship with it. I found comfort there because I didn't have to deal with any surprises. I knew what to expect from pain, I knew its voice. We spoke daily and I let it be what it wanted and do what it wanted. I didn't have to try hard with pain, but I also stopped growing, dreaming, and believing in God for anything besides what my pain was showing me.

Let's talk about it. We date our pain and then get into a relationship with it, a very toxic one. I want to help you get the courage to break up with your pain and inevitably your past. It's time to tell that pain and past "look I know we've been together for such a long time. You know me and I know you, but this just can't continue. You are holding me back and I can no longer be in a relationship with you. Deuces!" However you want to craft your break-up speech is up to you, but my friend, it is time to let it go. Feel free to use the line we all know so well, "it's not you, it's me!" God is doing a new thing in you at this very moment and you can't take that relationship with you okay? Now, just warning you, just like any natural human breakup you will go through a grieving period – the kind where you may want to cry and scarf down a bunch of ice cream. It doesn't feel good breaking up with something so familiar and even though it was hurting you it comforted you too (weird I know). You may even experience moments when you want to run back to what is familiar. Be patient with yourself.

I remember when I used to battle with self-harm. I would call myself breaking up with it and that would last for a couple of months; once it was over a year, but I just would always find myself back at it. When life would get hard and I would get depressed or sad I went back to what was familiar and what felt comforting and for me, that was self-harm (for you it may be a person, place, habit, etc.). It was such a toxic relationship but I was in it for such a long time until one day I decided to break up with it for good. Trust me I needed God for that too. I had to ask him to remove that relationship, burn it to the ground!

When I say break up with the pain and the past I do mean close the door, bolt that thang shut, burn it, whatever, but do not just 'ghost it'. For those of you who may not know that term, ghosting is when you just stop talking to someone abruptly, without notice, without closure. You just poof out of their lives no longer to be visible, like a ghost. But check this out, just because you can't see Casper does not mean he isn't there so in hindsight ghosting is never truly a resolution because it may be out of sight but it's not out of mind. Think about it, have you or someone you know ever ghosted someone or something but at some point, whether it's days, weeks, or years later, that person or thing resurfaces? (I'm raising my hand as I'm guilty, too). So yeah, let's not ghost the pain and past. We need a full-fledged break-up with a sound mind and a dead-set decision. Give yourself closure, give it to God and let the healing happen because God is doing a new thing and you can't take that pain with you to where he is leading you. Can I pray with you?

> *Dear Lord Jesus,*
>
> *You are the ultimate healer and chain breaker. There is none like You in all the earth and there is nothing You cannot do. Forgive us for staying in situations that were detrimental to our growth and relationship with You. Thank You for never turning Your back on us in moments we felt unworthy and allowed pain to dictate our lives. Lord, I come interceding on behalf of this reader who has a heart for you. Help them to break up with everything that is not of You. Everything that has made itself at home in our lives, I ask that You evict it swiftly. Less of them and all of You, Father. I thank You for what You are doing within them and around them at this very moment. Help them to continue pressing on and give them the strength to not go back to what is familiar, but instead call on You to be their strength. Thank You, Father, for hearing and answering this prayer.*
>
> *In Jesus' name,*
> *Amen.*

CHAPTER TAKEAWAYS

- *You must break up with your pain and not 'ghost' it.*
- *Painful habits can't live in the place God is taking you as they will become a hindrance to your re-birth.*
- *God is doing a new thing!*

Processing Time: Use this page to journal your thoughts, takeaways, etc.

_____

_____

_____

_____

_____

_____

_____

_____

_____

_____

_____

_____

_____

_____

_____

_____

_____

_____

_____

_____

_____

Fear

*"Fear not, for I am with you; be not dismayed, for I
am your God; I will strengthen you, I will help you,
I will uphold you with my righteous right hand."*

ISAIAH 41:10 (NIV)

As you continue journeying along with me and have officially broken up with your past and pain (not ghosted, right?), I want to address what you are going to experience or may be experiencing right now, and that's fear. Let's talk about it. The spirit of fear is crippling and God himself tells us that this overwhelming spirit did not come from Him (2 Timothy 1:7). If it did not come from God, then take a wild guess, who do you think it's coming from? You guessed correctly, the enemy who I call the ops. Remember the ops comes to steal, kill and destroy you by any means necessary and his biggest plot of all time is fear! By giving you the spirit of fear, he can literally freeze you in place. He will prevent you from moving any further, thus stealing your joy, killing your hopes, and destroying who God has called you to be. I struggled severely with the spirit of fear during my re-birth. What are you the most afraid of in this season of rebirthing? I can't answer that for you, but I can share some of the fears I had and how I overcame them. You may already feel this coming along, you should know me pretty well by now so go ahead and grab that journal and something to write with. Let's make a list of all the fears you currently have when it comes to this season of rebirth and breaking up with your pain and past. Here's mine:

My Re-birthing Fears
• Losing friends that I love.
• Not being able to bounce back from a loss.
• Failing and not being successful.
• Not getting it "right" and God becoming fed up with me.
• People from my past using my struggles with mental health and suicide against me.
• People judging and rejecting me.
• Never being good enough.

These were all of the fears that I let cripple me and God helped me realize that for me to fully experience this rebirth, letting go of these fears would be the toughest labor pains but he will be with me, so I must not fear. Just like a loved one holding the hand and reminding the mom in labor to breathe, God is right here with us. He is holding your hand through the pain and remember there is joy on the other side of labor.

I recall one of the hardest labor pains I was experiencing during my season of re-birth was having to deal with the opinions and treatment from others. I feared people. During my divorce and even after, I was dealing with friends who I love and who I once considered family rallying against me and using my past struggle with mental health as fuel. I legit was receiving phone calls and text messages about my dearest friends and ex-husband telling people I was mentally unstable. Those hurtful rumors and judgments were spreading like wildfire so much so it was even seeping into my career. There was an "Ebony is Crazy" committee formed and one of the members even shared the narrative with my direct supervisor in an effort to tarnish my credibility and reputation with the university I worked for. This committee was relentless, and I hate to admit it but I feared them. More specifically, I feared my past. I was functioning still fearful that my past struggles with mental health, suicide, depression, and infidelity were going to just pop up and destroy my life. It's like I was always holding my breath. Even though God was moving greatly in my life, I was healing, and blessings were flowing in one after another, this spirit sent by the enemy convinced me that it was all too good to be true and the moment is coming when the ground would crumble beneath my feet.

I share all this with you because I know I am not alone in having such a fear. You may even find yourself nodding in agreement while reading because many of us are guilty of being afraid of our past. I remember listening to a message from Mrs. Shavon Smith and she dropped a gem. She said, "God is not going back to your past for permission to bless you." Her words became instrumental in lifting off that spirit of fear and I hope her words along with my own can free you as well. God is not looking at our past saying "well I don't know if I should bless her/him. I don't know if I should forgive them or even pour out my love on them". Those are nothing but lies from the enemy with hopes to keep us functioning in fear. Now what God does say about us is that if we are in him then we are a NEW creation (2 Corinthians 5:17). So, my friend, you have a CLEAN slate with no reason to fear the past! And while you are basking in being a new creation there is more, he is also fighting for you! I did not go into vengeance mode against the people who were speaking ill of me and ruining my reputation (believe me it was hard. I'm saved but still human). I turned it all over to God because vengeance is not mine. God then brought me back to what it says in His Word: "Those who worked against you will end up empty-handed—nothing to show for their lives. When you go out looking for your old adversaries you won't find them—Not a trace of your old enemies, not even a memory. That's right. Because I, your God, have a firm grip on you and I'm not letting go. I'm telling you, 'Don't panic. I'm right here to help you'" (Isaiah 41:10-11, MSG). I began praying for the committee instead and also then praying for God to remove the spirit of fear I was carrying. Please know that as long as you are connected to God, YOU WILL PROSPER. Can I pray for you?

Dear Lord Jesus,

You are Alpha and Omega. Whatever You speak comes to pass and You breathe life into dead places. You can do anything but fail. Forgive us for all the times we allowed the ploy of the enemy to take precedence in our lives. Forgive us for allowing fear to dictate who we are, who we become, and where we journey to. Thank You for Your forgiveness, Lord. Thank You for a clean slate and for making us a new creation. Lord, I come interceding on behalf of this reader. Allow the chains of fear to be broken off of their lives. Break each shackle gripped to their ankles and give them full mobility. Equip them with the tools they will need to conquer the spirit of fear that the enemy sends their way. Continue to fight on their behalf, Lord, and help them to join forces with You. In the name of Jesus, all attacks sent by the enemy must return to the pits of hell where they came from. Father, wipe their tears, dust them off, renew their minds and give them the endurance to run this race without fear. Thank you, Lord!

In Jesus' name,
Amen.

CHAPTER TAKEAWAYS

- Fear is a tactic and spirit sent by the enemy to keep you in bondage and stop your growth.
- You have no reason to fear. God is with you!
- God fights for us and vengeance is always His, not ours.
- As long as you are connected to God, you will prosper!

Processing Time: Use this page to journal
your thoughts, takeaways, etc.

_____

_____

_____

_____

_____

_____

_____

_____

_____

_____

_____

_____

_____

_____

_____

_____

_____

_____

The Recipe for
Ultimate Healing

"Do not be anxious or worried about anything, but in every situation, by prayer and petition, with thanksgiving, present your (specific) requests to God. and the peace of God which transcends all understanding is yours."

PHILIPPIANS 4:6-7 (NIV)

efore we dive into this next chapter, I want to say that I am so proud of you. If you have no one around you to support you through this season, just know I'm here with you. Keep pressing forward. I promise you have the strength to get through this and I know for a fact you are going to see a difference in your life. I sure did.

Now, let's keep journeying along. I don't know about you but the list I made in chapter 4, of all the things I was hiding, is heavy stuff! At first, I did not know where to start and I was even burdened by the contents of my list. It made me want to run and hide even more! I had no choice but to walk out this faith thing and request help and healing from God. Healing, let's talk about it. Healing is defined as "the process of making or becoming sound or healthy again." Let's pause and zoom in on that word 'again'. Hmmm, the word again that appears in this definition gave me an epiphany. When God created us, we were already healthy and whole. That means if I need healing then I can't go to God as if I am asking for something new to be added to me to make me a better person but instead, I need Him to strip away the things that He never gave me. The things that were never mine to keep. I was born whole and healthy but I picked up some unhealthy things along the way. I picked up fear, insecurities, bitterness and so many lies along the way (i.e my list) and none of that belongs to me. What have you picked up along the way? Time to return to sender! If God tells us it's not from him (example: 2 Timothy 1:7) then who is it from? Well, this sender has many names: the devil, enemy, ops, etc. Send all that mess back to where it belongs and let's embrace the healing that comes from it. More specifically, God can heal you but you have to stop hiding. Be honest, tell him how you picked up some extra baggage and mess along your journey through this life and you don't want it anymore. He's waiting to hear from you through prayer.

I remember years ago being taught how to pray by my older cousin while she was leading children's Sunday school. Mind you, I was years older than the toddlers she was teaching, but I was a student right with them and learned the A.C.T.S acronym of prayer. This helped me learn that there is a formula for prayer (it blew my mind). This has guided me when learning how to go to my father in prayer. Let's review it together:

HOW	TO	PRAY
A	**Adoration**	*Tell Jesus how wonderful he is and how much you love him*
C	**Confession**	*Confess any sins and cry out your weaknesses, pain, and brokenness*
T	**Thanksgiving**	*Thank Jesus for his forgiveness and all the things in your life he has done*
S	**Supplication**	*Ask God for all that you need for yourself and others. Make your request specific*

I'm still always learning how to pray. I remember I came across a devotional that taught me another acronym (I love acronyms, can't you tell?) This acronym was H.S.P.E (like High school P.E, helps me remember) the devotional gave these letters new meaning. It taught me how to have a heart posture for prayer and how we must go to Him **humbly** (realizing

I'm not God and I need him), specifically (being detailed in my needs), persistently (continuing firmly), and with expectancy (believing He will answer my prayer). So, I encourage you to write down H.S.P.E and A.C.T.S in your journal and also on sticky notes that can be placed in visible places so you can practice this because remember it takes 21 days for something to become a habit.

I'm still praying for you, but it's long overdue for you to also pray for yourself. God loves hearing your voice. Let's put this thang in motion. Use this processing time for writing out your own prayer.

CHAPTER TAKEAWAYS

- Prayer is where we find the ultimate healing and connect with God.
- Pray using A.C.T.S. = Adoration, Confession, Thanksgiving, and Supplication.
- Pray H.S.P.E. = Humbly, Specifically, Persistently, and with Expectancy.
- Make prayer a lifestyle.

Processing Time: Use this page to journal your thoughts, takeaways, etc.

_____

_____

_____

_____

_____

_____

_____

_____

_____

_____

_____

_____

_____

_____

_____

_____

_____

_____

_____

_____

8

The Shift

"Now to Him who is able to do exceedingly abundantly above all that we ask or think, according to the power that works in us."

EPHESIANS 3:20 (NIV)

*Y*ou are doing amazing. Look at you praying, believing, and trusting God. I know it may not feel very good right now, but keep pressing on. You may find yourself vulnerable and even crying a bit more than you are used to, but don't forget your tools. Flip back to that prescription in chapter two to make sure you are following the doctor's orders. God is such a great physician and even on your tough days just know they are temporary because joy is right around the corner. Find your rhythm and continue to follow your new routine. You got this!

Now, as you continue to pray and grab your healing there is going to be a shift. A shift, let's talk about it. I don't feel good having to tell you this but it's necessary for your re-birth: you are getting ready to lose some people that you love, possessions that you may feel you can't live without, and habits that you have grown to admire. Just take a breath. I know that is a lot to swallow. For some of you, this news may make you excited- you might have even said to God "let's do it! I want to clean house!" For others, you may be feeling more of what I felt which was sadness, fear, and worry. You may be saying to God, "But I love them, I love these things, please let me have it. Just work around it." Try your hardest not to look at the shift as defeat and a loss. Allow God to create space.

I remember when I first was going through my divorce and I was speaking with my therapist, running down all the things I knew would be changing and all of the fears I had of the things that I did not want to change. I was a mess. I knew I did not need to endure the marriage anymore, but I could not fathom the thought of divorce and definitely not moving out of my house. I prided myself in being a homeowner and my house gave me so much in my mind. It was where I hosted a bunch of parties, and barbecues and it was a getaway for my friends at the time. I loved my kitchen and the security I felt in having a place I could call my own, but I had to let it go. I know it might sound silly and materialistic to some but letting that go hurt. So those were my first two losses and I thought the house and the marriage were the only things I was going to lose in that season. I had no idea that God wanted to create even more space in my life and I was caught off guard by the losses that came next. I began to then lose friends and not just any friends. These were friends I knew for about fifteen years. Friends I considered sisters and who I told God (here I went again telling Him what to do) were going to be in my life forever. The heartbreak that came with that felt worse than the marriage that ended. No one ever really talks about how friendship breakups can be more painful and life-altering than any breakup with a significant other. By that time, I was distraught and thought, "God, what in the world is happening?" Of course, now I can say to you that I see He was creating space, but at the time when things were happening back-to-back (within weeks might I add), I saw everything as a loss and defeat. I then began to lose more. I lost my credibility and reputation amongst people who I valued. Unfortunately, I had to file a restraining order against my ex-husband which caused a field day of chaos. Individuals who I considered friends and even family began to attack me for filing that order. The next thing I know, people are using my past struggles with depression and mental health against me and began labeling me as crazy and insane. Can you imagine the conversation I then had to have with God? I felt broken. I was finalizing a divorce, so that marriage was gone, but my best friends were also gone, and then stones were simultaneously being thrown as people I loved labeled and judged me.

I was not prepared for such losses because I had already crafted my life plan with a mind made up to fulfill it on my terms. I share this with you not to speak ill of any of these people because I will forever have love for them, but I share this to keep it real with you about some of the losses that you will experience in this season so they do not come as a surprise. I want you to really understand that what God is doing in your life requires more space. He is going to have to get rid of some people and things you love just so He can swoop in and bless you exceedingly and abundantly far more than you can think or imagine. If you want Him to do a new thing, He has to remove some old things. Everyone and everything can't go where He is taking you. Now, I know that was a bit heavy, but are you ready for the good news? He will replace everything you may lose in this season. The even better news is that He will not only replace it but multiply it (hits a happy dance)!

As I consistently followed his prescription and made time to meet with Him, God began to flood my life with more than I could possibly imagine. He replaced my old house with a new one that is bigger and better. He replaced those friendships by giving me a village of people who genuinely love and support me without judgment and selfish gain. He healed me from shame and lifted off every title given to me by those who hurt me. He replaced all I "lost" and then gave more (this is where the exceedingly and abundantly comes in). He then gave me a new state, city, and leadership position at one of the top universities in the nation! He then gave me a contract as a freelance writer for a great company and made me a published author. He also gave me love. Lastly, He gave me a joy that I honestly can't put into words. I can't go without mentioning that all of this happened to me in less than a year! God is continuing to BLOW. MY. MIND. I decree and declare in the mighty name of Jesus that He will do the same for you! Let's pray together:

Dear Lord Jesus,

Thank you for being who You are in our lives. You are the ultimate healer, protector, and comforter. You reign and no one is above You. Forgive us, Lord, for the moments when we doubt Your plan and presence in our lives. Forgive us for fighting You and desiring to have things our way. Forgive us, Lord for the moments we are not proud of. Thank You, Father, for your forgiveness, grace, and mercy. Thank you for never treating us as our sins deserve. Thank you for continuously wiping the slate clean. Lord, I come interceding on behalf of this reader. I pray that you provide them comfort and peace during this shift in their lives. Lord, give them peace in knowing that your divine plan is far better than they can even imagine and that the growing pains they are feeling are necessary and temporary. Thank You for the exceedingly and abundantly that is on the way. Father, I am asking that you show up and show out in their lives. Give them a testimony that will display just how amazing, powerful, and loving you are. Thank You, Father, for what is to come. We love you.

In Jesus' name,
Amen

CHAPTER TAKEAWAYS

- God will need to create space in your life so be prepared to lose some people, possessions, etc. Not everything and everyone can go to where you are headed.
- God promises that he will give us exceedingly and abundantly, far more than we can ever imagine! Lean into that promise daily and know everything will work out far better!
- Give God a chance to blow your mind!

*Processing Time: Use this page to journal
your thoughts, takeaways, etc.*

Forgiveness

*"In Him we have redemption through His blood, the
forgiveness of sins, according to the riches of His grace which
He made to abound toward us in all wisdom and prudence."*

EPHESIANS 1:7-8 (NIV)

et's talk about forgiveness. I thought the only forgiveness I had to give was towards my former friends, ex-husband, and family members but then God sat me down and told me that there is more forgiveness he needs me to give. God silenced my thoughts and asked, "Ebony, when did you stop trusting me?" I was appalled and offended by God's question. I couldn't believe he was accusing me of not trusting him. I began saying to him "God don't you see me following your directions? I'm getting up early, I'm listening to the sermons, I'm tithing, but you still say I'm not trusting you. I don't get it!" It was at that moment that God spoke. He said "daughter, how can you trust me if you have yet to forgive me?" (Whew, I was shook!) He took me back in time.

When I was a little girl, at the age of six or seven I cursed God. During this time, I was experiencing severe turmoil, confusion, and heartbreak. By that age, I'd already experienced rape and molestation. I also was experiencing a lot of disappointment and abandonment. This moment from the past plays so vividly in my mind that I can see the room I was standing in, feel the emotions that I felt, and hear the question "why God?" I can even see my little hands. I remember sticking my thumb up and saying "God, you don't deserve a thumbs up! This thumbs-up is not for You even if it is facing the sky. Just know that every moment forward You get a thumbs down and the devil gets a thumbs up. You aren't a nice God, and You lie, and You don't love me. So, no more thumbs up for you. I hate You, God. Devil, I love you." I then walked out of that room and went on about my business. I was only a child so I did not know the magnitude of what took place that day. But even still, God never took His hands off of me. Even when I got older in my preteen years and gave my life to God and got baptized, I see now that I never truly let go of those words I spoke to Him that day. Even though I would sing His praises and thank Him, there was still that little girl who was angry with God and had some unfinished business buried deep down. That little girl never forgave God for the terrible things she experienced.

I challenge you in the same way God challenged me. When did you stop trusting Him? Sit with that question. Think beyond your most recent hurt. Go back in time. I had to go back to the age of six. I strongly believe that your ultimate healing and prosperity lie in finding that answer. Once God gave me the answer to this question, everything changed. I finally experienced true healing and restoration. God knows I was a child who was enduring a lot of hurt, abandonment, and pain. Of course, He knew what He was doing and how everything would serve a purpose, but at that time I did not. He never took me cursing Him seriously, but He knew the impact it was going to have on me spiritually from that moment forward. He knew that I would always get to a point in my walk with Him when I would say no. I would say *there's no way I'm doing that. There's no way I'm taking that type of leap of faith. I can't trust that things will work out.* It all goes back to that six-year-old Ebony who stopped trusting God and now decades later, the woman I became to be was still living in that distrust from such a long time ago.

I say to you now that there is freedom on the other side of trusting God. I'm not sure when you started to doubt that He is good, He loves you, and He has plans for you to prosper. But I can tell you this: every promise He makes is true. It's just that as a little girl I was so angry with

God for what happened to me and what was happening at that time in my adolescent life that I made a subconscious decision to only trust God to a certain extent. I treated Him as if He were a man. Subconsciously I made it up in my mind that He could only get me so far and that He can only be trusted but so much because He allowed pain in my life. And because He allowed me to experience pain at such a young age, I took that as Him not being faithful. So, every time I experienced hardship in my life, I would hold it against God and use that as a way to validate why He can't be fully trusted. I then put my faith in myself. I took on the declaration of "me, myself, and I". I put my faith in my work ethic, my accomplishments in school, my degrees, my job, my bank account, and even in other people, all before him. I hope this is hitting you in the same way it hit me. It came full force like a tractor-trailer at full speed to my chest and it did not feel good. But it was necessary because I finally got my breakthrough and I know you can too. I would like to pray for you:

Dear Lord Jesus,

You are so faithful. You are powerful and there is none like You. You are omniscient. You are perfect in all your ways. Forgive us father for not trusting you fully. Forgive us for putting You in a box and placing limits on You. Forgive us for the moments when You desired full access to us and we turned away from You. Forgive us for putting our trust in the world and not in You. Thank You for Your forgiveness, patience, and guidance. Lord, I come interceding on behalf of this reader. Lord, speak to their hearts and spirit. Allow them to realize when they stopped trusting You. Place in them a heart of forgiveness. Help them to forgive You and learn how You never intended to hurt them and that You never left or stopped loving them. Help them to forgive themselves and remove all shame. Fill them up Lord with Your love and may it radiate throughout their lives. Thank you, Lord, for the breakthrough they are experiencing at this very moment. Hold them close. We love You.

In Jesus' name,
Amen.

CHAPTER TAKEAWAYS

- Identify when you stopped fully trusting God and talk to Him about it. He's been waiting.
- God's love for us is deeper than any ocean and He never stops loving us.
- God needs you to trust His plans even when you don't understand. Seek Him consistently and He will give you all you need to continue your journey.

Processing Time: Use this page to journal
your thoughts, takeaways, etc.

_____

_____

_____

_____

_____

_____

_____

_____

_____

_____

_____

_____

_____

_____

_____

_____

_____

_____

_____

_____

Full-Circle

"And we know that for those who love God all things work together for good, for those who are called according to his purpose."

ROMANS 8:28 (NIV)

*B*efore we took our first breath, God knew us. He knew every part of our personality, every hair on our heads, and what our parents would name us. God even knew all the moments that would make us smile and every moment that would make us cry. He knew the community we would grow up in, the adversities that would arise, and the people who would cross our paths. You better believe that He even knew you would be reading this book on this day at this time and in this season of your life. God is all-knowing and He is faithful. He creates full-circle moments (our last SJR gem). Full-circle moments can be defined as such: "After a long series of events or changes, the same situation that you started with still exists." This means that even after all you encounter on life's journey thus far, the same child God created you to be when He formed you in your mother's womb still exists. You may have buried him or her, but who God ordained you to be and the plans He has for your life have never stopped existing.

My re-birth is nothing more than a full-circle moment. It is when God puts all the pieces together, including the good things, the bad things, all of the things I was hiding, and everything I wrote out on that list. That innocence that was taken away from me at a tender age is the innocence God had me tap back into. In the end, it drew me closer to Him. I instantly became that child running into the arms of her Daddy. He took the rape, abandonment, divorce, infidelity, etc., and worked it together for my good!

Let's talk about the good. I don't want you walking away thinking the good is the career, love, house, and friends He gave me. Those are just the icing and cherry on top, but the good is the re-birth. The good is the joy I now have that no one can take away. The good is what came out of everything I had to journey through. I am not the same broken, hurt, bitter, and insecure person. He changed me from the inside out! He still is not finished with me yet and my story (and yours) does not end with the breakthrough and triumph because more full-circle moments are awaiting. I'm excited for your testimony to unfold! Promise me one thing: that you will not keep it to yourself. I hope my story helped you, now go, bless another, and enjoy the journey. Let's pray:

> *Dear Lord,*
>
> *We adore You. You are the head of our lives and the light of our path. You are the beginning and the end. We praise Your name. Father, forgive us for sins we have committed knowingly and unknowingly. Wash us clean and renew our minds. Thank You for always forgiving us and showing up for us. Thank You for seeing us through every season of our lives. We thank You, Lord, for speaking through the pages of this book. I pray that Your words take root in the lives of every reader. May they be blessed and everyone attached to them as well. May Your plans for their lives be fulfilled. Help them to walk into this new season without shame, guilt, fear, or anything that is not of you. Lord, I pray that they continue diving deep into their relationship with You and that You would continue doing a great work in them. Even when the weapons form against them, I pray that the power that lives inside of them*

rises and defeats all plans of the enemy. His weapons won't prosper, but Your plans for them will. I thank You for their testimonies, breakthroughs, and triumphs. This is only the beginning and for that, I say thank You, Lord. Thank You, Father, for using me as an instrument and I pray that you are pleased. May every reader feel Your presence right where they are. Thank You for all You have already done, what You are doing right now, and what You are going to do. Have Your way. We love You and we trust You, Lord.

In Jesus' name,
Amen.

*Processing Time: Use this page to journal
your thoughts, takeaways, etc.*

Helpful
Scriptures for
the Journey

- "Before I formed you in the womb I knew you, before you were born I set you apart; I appointed you as a prophet to the nations." Jeremiah 1:5 (NIV)
- "For I know the plans I have for you, declares the LORD, plans to prosper you and not to harm you, plans to give you hope and a future." Jeremiah 29:11 (NIV)
- "Have I not commanded you? Be strong and courageous. Do not be afraid; do not be discouraged, for the Lord your God will be with you wherever you go." Joshua 1:9 (NIV)
- "But he said to me, 'My grace is sufficient for you, for my power is made perfect in weakness.' Therefore, I will boast all the more gladly about my weaknesses, so that Christ's power may rest on me." 2 Corinthians 12:9 (NIV)
- "Remember not the former things, nor consider the things of old. Behold, I am doing a new thing, now it springs forth, do you not perceive it?" Isaiah 43:18-19 (NIV)
- "Fear not, for I am with you; be not dismayed, for I am your God; I will strengthen you, I will help you, I will uphold you with my righteous right hand." Isaiah 41:10 (NIV)
- "Do not be anxious or worried about anything, but in every situation, by prayer and petition, with thanksgiving, present your (specific) requests to God. and the peace of God which transcends all understanding is yours" Philippians 4:6-7 (NIV)
- "Now to Him who is able to do exceedingly abundantly above all that we ask or think, according to the power that works in us." Ephesians 3:20 (NIV)
- "In Him, we have redemption through His blood, the forgiveness of sins, according to the riches of His grace which He made to abound toward us in all wisdom and prudence." Ephesians 1:7-8 (NIV)

- "And we know that for those who love God all things work together for good, for those who are called according to his purpose." Romans 8:28 (NIV)
- "Trust in the Lord with all your heart and lean not on your own understanding; in all your ways submit to him, and he will make your paths straight." Proverbs 3:5-6 (NIV)
- "The Lord is my light and my salvation— whom shall I fear? The Lord is the stronghold of my life—of whom shall I be afraid? When the wicked advance against me to devour me, it is my enemies and my foes who will stumble and fall. Though an army besiege me, my heart will not fear; though war break out against me, even then I will be confident." Psalm 27:1-3 (NIV)
- "I praise you because I am fearfully and wonderfully made; your works are wonderful; I know that full well." Psalm 139:14 (NIV)
- "No, in all these things we are more than conquerors through him who loved us." Romans 8:37 (NIV)
- "I can do all this through him who gives me strength." Philippians 4:13 (NIV)
- "Call to me and I will answer you and tell you great and unsearchable things you do not know." Jeremiah 33:3 (NIV)
- "Remain in me, as I also remain in you. No branch can bear fruit by itself; it must remain in the vine. Neither can you bear fruit unless you remain in me." John 15:4 (NIV)
- "Cast all your anxiety on him because he cares for you." 1 Peter 5:7 (NIV)
- "The LORD himself goes before you and will be with you; he will never leave you nor forsake you. Do not be afraid; do not be discouraged." Deuteronomy 31:8-9 (NIV)

References

1. *Jesus, I Have Prayed The Salvation Prayer.* Retrieved 2 April 2022 from https://hillsong.com/jesus/.
2. "Rebirth." Merriam-Webster Dictionary. Retrieved 2 April 2022 from https://www.merriam-webster.com/dictionary/be%20re-born#:~:text=%3A%20to%20be%20born%20again%20%3A%20to,reborn%20from%20its%20own%20ashes.

www.ingramcontent.com/pod-product-compliance
Lightning Source LLC
Chambersburg PA
CBHW020324130626
46549CB00003B/1008